Wandering Woman: Wyoming

The Ultimate Road Trip: One Woman's Journey Across the United States by Car

Julie Bettendorf

Contents

Introduction

"Not all who wander are lost."

Are you sure? I thought to myself, as I tried not to panic. I was a long way from anything familiar, but that was how it should be. I had driven thousands of miles on dusty, pothole-filled roads. It's often on the worst roads that you can discover something truly amazing.

My dusty CRV was parked beside me, containing one restless dog and a variety of snack bags, all empty by now. There were no buildings in sight, no cars or people or movement at all. Only the constant humming of the insects as they buzzed around my head.

I turned to my left – another straight road that trailed off into the distance. I glanced over to the right, then behind me – two more barely discernible roads stretched out into the abyss. I was in a four-way intersection with no signs, no sense of direction, and no sign of life for several miles. No cell service either. *Damn*, I thought. *I'm lost.*

How did I get here? I couldn't help but feel like this little intersection was a cruel metaphor for life. I began to daydream, imagining each road might transport me back to a different time, a different role in my life, and a different me.

If I took the road from whence I came, it could lead me all the way back to Oregon, back to my cheating third husband, back to a life of loneliness and solitude. There is no greater loneliness than being married to someone who isn't actually present in your life.

If I took the road to my left, perhaps it could take me back to my career as a dental hygienist, a job I hated deep down in my soul. There is something so disengaging about cleaning teeth for a living. It's a disgusting, smelly way to get a paycheck. It pays well, which is great, but the best part is the huge gob of friends I enjoy to this day.

Or maybe the road to my right, *yes – maybe that's the path*, I imagined. Maybe it could take me back to my real treasure, my kids. Back to their smiling, innocent faces as toddlers, as they danced around the Christmas tree and their father and I were still married. Back when they still needed me for every little thing.

But, that was just it. I didn't feel needed anymore. My kids weren't toddlers anymore – they were both full-grown adults, and far too busy for me. My dental buddies were still working, but I wasn't. Dental hygiene had robbed me of the cartilage in my fingers, giving me severe, disabling arthritis. And, I wouldn't be returning to any more husbands either, because three marriages were quite enough for me.

All three of these paths, all three of these roles – the wife, the mother, and the dental hygienist – had seemingly been stripped from me within a year. I was lost and looking to find myself again.

The funny thing about this phrase, "not all who wander are lost" – is that, in my experience, wandering and being lost walk hand-in-hand with one another, and the expression can be flipped. In my experience, not all who are lost are wandering, and that is a real disservice to the beauty and clarity that the world has to offer.

When one becomes lost, wandering is the only option to guide oneself back to a path. After all, one could not come upon any dirt path at all without wandering.

I began wandering at an early age, both with my mind and with my feet. At eight years old, I was reading a book about archaeology and dreaming of one day seeing Egypt. I didn't follow a traditional path in high school either, going heavily into foreign languages, in hopes of one day using them.

At twenty-five years old, I divorced my first husband (the dental student who talked me into becoming a dental hygienist so I could work for him) and decided to give traveling a real shot. I took off for the Andes and Macchu Picchu, climbing up ancient Inca stone steps to reach the magnificent ruins.

Anyone who has been to Macchu Picchu will tell you there is something ethereal and deeply spiritual about the place. The ruins stretch out across the emerald green mountains, way up in the middle of the sky. Macchu Picchu gave me my first experience of feeling history. This trip inspired me to come back and complete a degree in archaeology, and I've been wandering ever since.

More travel followed including a backpack trip around Europe for three months, by myself, and trips to Britain, Italy, and Greece. I visited the burial places of Crusaders, mummies, and ancient kings. I happened upon the castle of my namesake in Bettendorf, Luxembourg, and wandered my way through European history.

My favorite excursion by far was finally seeing Egypt with my daughter in 2012. Just like my childhood dream envisioned, I rode a camel beneath the pyramids of Giza, with my head wrapped in some man's sweaty turban. It was perfect.

Traveling has always been my own personal antidote to pain. I went to Mexico after my first and second divorces, Canada after my third, and Italy after my dad died. Call it avoidance if you want, but I call it an accelerated form of healing in the purest sense of the word. I believe travel can heal your soul.

Wandering has always worked its wonders on me – made me feel renewed, rejoiceful, grateful, and purposeful. It's been my medicine.

So, as I stood in that intersection, I once again wondered how wandering had led me so astray this time. *What the hell am I supposed to do now?* It was then that I realized that one last path had not been considered yet – the path which stretched straight out in front of me. *Which role does this represent?* I pondered.

The answer smacked me in the face.

That last dirt road – the only path that could take me where I wanted to go, the only path that ever truly healed me or showed me the way – was the path of the traveler. The wife, the mother, and the hygienist roles – though valued in their time – were sitting in the bleachers now. It was time to welcome and enable my boldest, bravest, and perhaps most pivotal role yet:

The role of the Wandering Woman.

Welcome to Wandering Woman

This book is for you – the grieving empty nester mom, the begrudged housewife, the woman in need of a drastic change in her life. Really, this book is for anyone with a passion for traveling. If you feel lost with no sense of direction or purpose in life, that's a bonus – this book will be even more appealing to you. And lastly, if you're a man reading this book, congratulations for holding a book with the word woman in the title. You're contributing to gender equality, and that's pretty neat.

I decided to combine three of my dearest loves – travel, history, and archaeology – and put them into a book because I believe wandering has the power to change your life. I have been to many areas of the world and had too many outstanding experiences to list. However, by the time both my children had

Me

moved out in 2017, I had never seen my own country – America. It was the perfect time to explore a new country (my own) and discover a new me at the same time.

So, I packed up my Honda CRV, along with some gear and my 14-year-old furry friend, Sadie. *Wandering Woman* is the chronicle of my journey across eleven states, discovering the joy of getting lost and finding myself along the way.

Why America?

A *merica, the beautiful?* I sure think so, but I didn't realize just how beautiful our country is until I embarked on traveling across eleven western states in a year.

The United States offers everything for the discerning palate. From spectacular beaches, austere mountains, to rolling plains, our country has it all. It's difficult to comprehend just how large and impressive our scenery is, until you experience it first-hand, with the ultimate road trip.

I also realized just how much of our history is missing from U.S. history I was taught as a kid. The history of our country didn't begin with the pilgrims landing on Plymouth Rock in the 1600s. Our history is far more ancient, with rock art and archaeological sites dating back over 12,000 years.

We also owe a tremendous debt to early pioneers who tamed our land. The Mormons and other groups ventured into the great unknown with their families and their worldly possessions. Some of them pulled cumbersome handcarts across the country to settle in inhospitable, dangerous locations.

The goal of Wandering Woman is to bring history back to life and make it interesting again. I am presenting some famous sites, and many little-known ones. You will take the road-less-traveled with me, while we explore ghost towns, rock art sites, archaeological sites, and museums, to discover the colorful tapestry that is our country.

I present some history, including dates, but my goal is to present more of the real-life stories of history, including ghost stories, profiles in history, voices from the past, and moments in time, to give you, the reader, a deeper understanding of the context of history.

This is by no means an exhaustive list of places to visit. In fact, I encourage you to discover America for yourself, as I did, by making a trek across the land by car. You can explore as the early explorers did, just a little more comfortably, with a lot less hardship.

I hope you enjoy this book and take a little time out to discover our beautiful country, and maybe even discover yourself in the process.

Safe Travels,

Julie Bettendorf

Welcome to Wyoming

The Cowboy State

*W*yoming is untamed country, with wide open spaces as far as the eye can see. If you have the wanderlust and want to just get up and head out, Wyoming is the place for you. Friendly people, abundant wildlife, and unique historical sites all combine in Wyoming, to create a fascinating, beautiful destination.

5 things to love about Wyoming:

The old military history sites at Fort Bridger, Fort Laramie, and Fort Caspar

The small herds of pronghorn antelope scattered throughout the plains

The frontier history in old ghost towns like South Pass City and Miner's Delight

The living history museums in places like Old Trail Town in Cody

The dinosaur evidence in places like Fossil Butte and Wyoming Dinosaur Center

Dreams of Wyoming

*"I'm fortunate to live in Wyoming, one of the most beautiful, pristine places in the world." -**John Barrasso***

*"My favorite part of Wyoming is as soon as I hit the border. I'm home, where life is good." -**Rulon Gardner***

"I don't know if it's just my age or the climate or the high altitude or some of those old-cowboy values rubbing off on me, but I've grown slightly mellower living in Wyoming. I think if you ride into the

West on a high horse, you pretty soon end up in a pile of manure."
-Alexandra Fuller

Top Stuff to See in Wyoming

Favorite Wyoming Ghost Towns:

- Miner's Delight

- South Pass City

Favorite Wyoming Archaeological Sites:

- Legend Rock

- Independence Rock

Favorite Wyoming Historical Sites:

- Register Cliff

- Fort Laramie

Favorite Wyoming Museums:

- Old Trail Town, Cody

- Wyoming Dinosaur Center, Thermopolis

When driving in Wyoming, watch out for:

Bison, pronghorn antelope, prairie dogs, and wild turkeys

Early Wyoming

Soldiers at Fort Laramie

Early Visitors to Register Cliff

Early Fossil Hunters at Fossil Butte

Northern Wyoming

Medicine Lodge Creek

Cody

*C*ody has a wonderful outdoor museum called ***Old Trail Town.*** The museum was begun in 1967 by Bob Edgar, a Wyoming native and archaeologist. It's a fascinating collection of 27 buildings dating from 1879 to 1901. There are at least one hundred horse drawn vehicles, and a massive collection of old west artifacts and memorabilia.

I was lucky enough to visit twice, once in the pouring rain, when all the buildings were closed, and then again, in full sunshine when the buildings were open.

It's a wonderful place, complete with many old wagons.

Curly's cabin was built in 1885, and belonged to Custer's Crow Indian scout named Curly.

Curly survived the Battle of the Little Bighorn on June 25, 1876, and came back to deliver news of Custer's defeat.

Hole in the Wall cabin was built in 1883.

It was used by Butch Cassidy, the Sundance Kid, and members of his gang.

The ***Rivers Saloon*** was built by Henry Rivers in 1888.

It was a favorite hangout of Butch Cassidy and other outlaws and cowboys.

Bullet holes can be seen in the door.

The ***Morrison cabin*** was built in 1884 by Luther Morrison.

He was an early sheep farmer who came out west on the Oregon Trail in 1853.

The ***Buffalo Hunter's cabin*** was built in 1880 by Jim White and Oliver Hanna.

Jim White was murdered at the hunting camp on Shell Creek in late October 1880.

There are many other historic buildings, including the *Coffin School*, built in 1884.

It was named for Alfred Nower, who died of gangrene in the cabin in 1885. He chopped himself in the leg while cutting logs.

Other buildings include the ***Bonanza Post Office***, built in 1885,

and the ***Shell Store***, built in 1892.

It was the first store in Wyoming.

Old Trail Town has some interesting burials too, including:

*Jim White, the buffalo hunter,
1828-1880*

*Jeremiah Johnston, frontiers-
man, 1824-1900*

*Phillip Vetter, a trapper killed by
a grisly bear, 1855-1892*

Jack Stilwell, frontiersman and scout, 1850-1903

*W.A. Gallagher and Blind Bill, two cowboys who were murdered
in 1894*

Belle Dreary, the Woman in Blue, murdered in Arland, 1867-1897

How to get to Old Trail Town:

Old Trail Town is located at 1831 Demaris Drive, in Cody.

Profiles in history:

Buffalo Bill Cody started out working as an express messenger when he was a young boy, and graduated to a Pony Express rider. During the Civil War, when he was just sixteen, he became a scout with the Kansas Volunteers. After the Civil War, Cody became the lead scout for General Sheridan and participated in several wars against Indians.

He also had a flair for acting, and in 1883, he began his famous Wild West tour, involving reenactments of famous battles and other Western lore. Annie Oakley and Sitting Bull joined the tour in

1885. The Wild West Tour became a popular staple in America and in Europe.

Buffalo Bill invested most of his considerable wealth in building the town of Cody, Wyoming, and wanted to be buried there. He died January 10, 1917, of kidney, heart, and prostate problems, while living with his sister in Denver. There wasn't enough money from his estate to bury him in Wyoming, so he was buried atop Lookout Mountain near Denver. Enss

Medicine Lodge

*M**edicine Lodge** is spectacular. There are hundreds of petroglyphs and pictographs etched and painted onto a sandstone cliff.

Many of the images are ancient, up to 2500 years old.

Many are also severely weathered, making them faint and difficult to see.

There are images of shield-bearing warriors, along with animal-shapes, including a pronghorn antelope, a large elk etching, grizzly bear, and a bison.

There are also images of sheet music and a violin from the historic, early-settler period of the 1800s, and historical graffiti from the early 1900s. ^{Wyoming Parks}

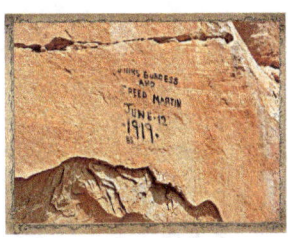

How to get Medicine Lodge:

Medicine Lodge is located at 4800 County Road 52, in Hyattville.

A word about petroglyphs and pictographs:

Petroglyphs were made by taking river rock and heating it and
then cooling it suddenly so it cracks to form a sharp tool. This tool
was used to chisel along with another stone for a hammer to peck
or incise the designs on rock. A thick desert coating called a patina
was removed to expose the lighter rock underneath.

Pictographs, are painted instead of incised. They are drawn pictures using minerals like hematite mixed with a binder such as animal fat, urine, or oil to make paint. The spiral sun symbol commonly represented may show Hopi migration, where they come from and where they have been. Pictograph colors are:

- Black, which is made with yellow ochre, pinon gum, and sumac

- Red, which is made with red ochre and mahogany root

- Yellow, which is made with rabbitbrush

- Plant oils and animal fats were used as binders

Devil's Tower

The ***Devil's Tower*** is a unique rock formation in Northeastern Wyoming. It is called Bear's Lodge by the Lakota, but it was named "Devils Tower" by Colonel Richard Dodge, who led a military expedition in 1875 into the Black Hills to confirm the discovery of gold. Europeans first climbed the formation on July 4, 1893, using a ladder made of oak pegs.

The igneous rock formation towers 867 feet above ground level and has a diameter of 1000 feet at its base. The Devil's Tower has the honor of being the world's first national monument, dedicated on September 24, 1906. Moulton, NPS

The top of the tower measures 1 .25 acres and is covered with native plants. Nothing can prepare you for the sheer size as you look up at it. Rather than view it from the highway, it's best to go inside the monument and view it to get a full perspective of how massive it is.

The wildlife is pretty great too, from the cute prairie dogs, to the wild turkeys strolling about.

How to get to Devil's Tower:

Devil's Tower is in Northeastern Wyoming, off Hwy. 110.

Voices from the past:

"*[The Tower's] remarkable structure, its symmetry, and its prominence made it an unfailing object of wonder...once seen, so singular and unique that it can never be forgotten.*" **Henry Newton, Assistant Geologist, Newton-Jenney Expedition, 1875.**

Central Wyoming

Miner's Delight

Fort Caspar

F*ort Caspar* started out as a trading post, founded by Louis
Guinard in 1859. Guinard also built a bridge, which was the

scene of a massacre of soldiers in 1865, including a Lt. Caspar Collins, for whom Fort Caspar is named.

The post also became a stage stop, pony express station, and a post office.

Fort Caspar remained in operation until 1867. Today, you can view buildings with interiors, which were reconstructed based upon sketches which Lt. Caspar Collins drew in 1863.

Buildings include a **_Sutler's Store_**, **_blacksmith shop_**, **_commissary_**, and **_officer's quarters_**. There is also an example of a **_Mormon ferry_**, used for river crossings. City of Casper

The **Visitor's Center** has a fine
collection of artifacts including
the head of an axe, a locket with
a lock of blonde hair inside, and
a metal arrowhead, which was
one of 50 removed from a sol-
dier's body. Other items include
surgical saws and other medical
equipment.

How to get to Fort Caspar:

Fort Caspar is located near the intersection of 13th Street and
Wyoming Boulevard in Caspar.

A word about Mormon ferries:

From 1836 to 1868, at least 350,000 emigrants used the Oregon, Mormon, and California trails to travel westward. One of the most time-consuming and dangerous parts of the trip were the river crossings. In 1847, Brigham Young and his party arrived in the area of Fort Caspar, then known as North Platte.

Young and some men of his party constructed a large ferry out of trees hollowed out like canoes, with wooden slabs for the floor. The ferry also had a rudder and two oars to steer it. The Mormons left behind to manage the ferry charged a cost of $1.50 per wagon to cross the river. Fort Caspar Museum

Independence
Rock

*I**ndependence Rock*** is an important landmark along the Oregon Trail, where pioneers and explorers camped, rested, and took time to carve their names in the rock. The landmark was named in 1830 by fur trappers who reached it on the Fourth of July. During the years 1843 through 1869, it is estimated almost 500,000 emigrants passed by Independence Rock.

Many of the names have been worn away by time, so they have been replaced with a bronze plaque to show who has been here.

Narcissa Whitman, who visited here in 1836, has a plaque too. She, and Eliza Hart Spalding, were the first white women in Wyoming, and the first women on the Oregon Trail. Narcissa and her husband made it all the way to Washington State to establish the Whitman Mission.

There are many very early names which are no longer visible including M.K. Hugh, in 1824, Hanna Snow, in 1844, G. Gingham, in 1846, J. Bower, in 1847, Milo Ayer, age 29, in 1849, and V .D. Moody, July 24, 1849. Among the many names are those of Brigham Young, who visited with his party in 1847. Moulton

How to get to Independence Rock:

Independence Rock is located 60 miles southwest of the City of Caspar, off Hwy. 220.

Voices from the past:

"...the names of all the travelers who have passed by are there to be read, written in coarse characters." **Pioneer priest Pierre-Jean DeSmet, 1841.** He christened the rock, "The Great Register of the Desert."

South Pass City

S outh Pass City, established in 1867, is at an important cross-roads, because the town marked an easy passage across the continental divide for travelers along the Oregon Trail.

Gold was found in 1867 on the Sweetwater River. It was called the Cariso (later Carissa) Lode.

Within a few years, South Pass City contained over 300 buildings including hotels, stores, butcher shops, a bowling alley, billiard hall, and multiple saloons. The town boasted a population of at least 2000 residents. Varney, Weis

There are over 30 historic buildings in excellent condition, including the *John & Lida Sherlock House* built in the 1890s, on land purchased for $1 by John's mother. In 2002, archaeologists found evidence of an earlier hotel on the site that had burned down in the 1870s.

The **E.A. Slack cabin** honors the first woman Justice of the Peace in the US-Esther Morris, and William Bright, legislator and suffrage supporter who helped make Wyoming the first state to let women vote. The cabin was owned by Edward Slack, Esther's son, who published the South Pass News.

The town also has a **refrigeration house**, which is a cave-built in 1868, to house perishable food and liquor, and also to protect the townspeople from Indian raids.

The **Sherlock barn** was built in the 1890s and archaeologists found at least one gun and whiskey bottles under the floor boards.

As you walk around the town, also look out for the *Carissa Saloon* built in the 1890s, *South Pass Hotel* built in 1868, and the *mercantile* built in the 1870s.

Other sites include the *Carissa Mine* and the *Sweetwater County Jail*, built in 1870 for $2000. The *Dance Hall* was built in the 1890s, and the *Libby Cabin*, which was built in 1899, was once an isolation hospital. Don't miss the *Exchange Saloon*, built in 1868, by John Swingle, who was the town's county commissioner, building contractor, saloon and stable owner, and undertaker.

One of my favorite buildings is the picturesque *schoolhouse* built in the 1890s. A little bit of schoolhouse lore concerns a former student who placed gunpowder in the teacher's pipe to get revenge on the teacher. Apparently, the teacher enjoyed whipping kids with a willow switch.

The ***Leckie House*** was the home of Andrew Leckie, who died by falling 80 feet down the mine shaft, and his older brother Sam, who was gunned down in a disagreement with a sheepherder. The small bridge in town is the ***Price Street Bridge***, named for Charles Price, the city's recorder in 1867. Price may  have helped plat the original South Pass City.

How to get to South Pass City:

South Pass City is located about 35 miles southwest of the town of Lander, off Hwy 28.

Profiles in history:

Esther Morris was born in 1814. She arrived in South Pass City in 1869 and supported suffrage and a woman's right to vote. She submitted her name for justice of the peace and was elected on Feb. 17, 1870. Esther was the first woman in the United States to hold public office. She served in office for 9 months in 1870, making rulings on civil and criminal cases. She left South Pass City and settled in Cheyenne, Wyoming. She died there in 1902.

A word about mail order brides:

The aftermath of the Civil War and the movement West for the Gold Rush led to a scarcity of men in the Eastern United States. The hardships of living in mining camps and prospecting was not a great environment for women either, so there were too many men and too few women in the West. Published numbers state the ratio was sometimes as great as 200 men to 1 woman. Business-minded people began what was known as the "mail-order bride" industry.

A well-read newspaper known as the Matrimonial News listed advertisements for women seeking to marry men, and for men seeking to marry women.

Here are two of the more striking examples of ads from January 1887:

"A good-looking young lady of 19, 5 feet 3 inches high, black hair and eyes, would like to find someone to love."

"I want to know some pretty girl of 17 to 20 years. I am 29, 5 feet 9 inches tall, a blonde: I can laugh for fifteen minutes and I want some pretty girl to laugh with me."

And from the New Plan Company Catalog, September 1917:

"Winsome Miss of 18 years, considered attractive looking, have many friends, very pleasant and lively, blue eyes, dark hair, fair complexion, good education, good cook and housekeeper, weight 130, height 5 feet; would make the right man a good wife; have a profit of $10,000; will answer all letters containing stamps."

"Would like to correspond with a farmer about 30 to 35 years old. Am an American widow of 33; height 5 feet, 2 inches; weight 200; brown eyes; brown hair; common school education. Personal property worth $1500. Object matrimony. No flirts need write."[Enss]

Miner's Delight

M*iner's Delight* is one of my favorite ghost towns. It's remote and quiet, and I was the only one walking around.

What's left of the town is in a spectacular setting, deep in the woods.

It began as Hamilton City, with the Miner's Delight Mine, where gold was found in 1867. The town was then named after the mine, and reached a peak population of 100 residents.

The town's life was short, with buildings being abandoned by 1907. Eight log cabins in a state of "arrested decay" are within the site. Varney, Weis

As you walk around Miner's Delight, look out for *"Cocktail Jimmy's Saloon."* James Kime (Jimmy) settled here in 1869, and became a state senator in 1892. He was the longest permanent resident of the town. Jimmy got his nickname from drinking with

friends late into the night, and
missing a crucial vote in the senate.

How to get to Miner's Delight:

Miner's Delight is located about 3 miles east of the town of Atlantic City, on Fort Stambaugh Road.

A word about preservation:

Many ghost towns are not restored. Instead, they undergo a process known as "arrested decay." The buildings are only repaired and stabilized, to prevent them from collapsing, but they are not restored.

Efforts are made to stabilize rock foundations and repair leaking roofs to prevent further damage, but the buildings are left in their original condition at the time of purchase.

Ghost story:

There is a legend about ***Tommyknockers*** that are said to haunt many mining camps. Tommyknockers got their name from Cornish miners who believed that little men lived underground and caused the knocking with their tiny hammers.

Some early miners believed Tommyknockers were good spirits who were warning of an impending mine collapse. Others believed that the person who heard the knocking would die. Still others believed that Tommyknockers were the spirits of miners who had died during a cave-in. Some miners even left offerings of food and drink to appease the Tommyknockers.

Thermopolis

Thermopolis is famous for its hot springs, and for the ***Wyoming Dinosaur Center***. It's one of the better dinosaur museums, containing well-curated fossils from many locations around the world.

There is an excellent repre-sentation of both small fossils and massive dinosaurs. Some are casts, but many are actual fossils, including this ammonite, which is over 200 million years old.

Some of my favorites include the fossilized crabs, graceful starfish, and the archaeopteryx, the only one on display in North Ameri-ca. The archaeopteryx is famous for having characteristics seen in both reptiles and birds.

Another one of my favorites is the unusual dunkleosteus, an apex predator which could grow up to 33 feet long. It was an efficient predator, with a bite strength of 11,000 pounds. It could cut its prey in half with a single bite.

The **Hot Springs National Park** is also in Thermopolis, and it contains the Wyoming State Bison Herd. The best time to see them is morning and evening. At one time, over 60 million bison roamed North America. Now, there are only about 31,000.

Wyoming Dinosaur Center

The park also contains a tiny pioneer cemetery, called the **Smoky Row Cemetery**. It got its name because of the smoke travelers would see as they approached the temporary dugouts residents were living in.

Burials continued in the cemetery until 1890.

How to get to the Wyoming Di-
nosaur Center and Hot Springs National Park :

The Wyoming Dinosaur Center is located at 110 Carter Ranch Rd,
and the Hot Springs National Park is located at 220 N Park St, both
in Thermopolis

Legend Rock

*L**egend Rock*** is wonderful. The site contains about 300 in-
dividual images, some of which have been carbon-dated to
11,000 years ago. The darker the image, the older the image is. The

darker images are believed to be early Archaic from 8000 BC to 6000 BC.

Many of the images are examples of the Dinwoody style of rock art. The Dinwoody style is found only in the Big Horn and Wind River Basins. The style is represented by large, human-like images with various numbers of fingers and toes.

The figures often wear elaborate headdresses and may have patterns of lines etched on their bodies. Headdresses are considered to be medicine or power among North American Indians.
Wyoming State Parks

There are also many whimsical animal figures, including my favorites, the bunnies.

The figures are fascinating and include a thunderbird, which represents power, and various human-like figures with other figures contained in them. These could represent pregnancy or spiritual helpers of the larger figures.

There are numerous figures spanning cracks in the rocks. This positioning may represent a transition from one dimension to another. The elk image represents "love medicine" among the Shoshone and Crow. The elk spirit can increase a warrior's strength, and aid in attracting a mate.

How to get to Legend Rock:

Legend Rock is located about 20 miles northwest of Thermopolis.

A word about petroglyphs:

Petroglyphs are pecked or incised into a rock surface, whereas pictographs are painted onto a rock surface. Petroglyphs can be of several types:

En toto, in which the entire image is pecked into the rock, or outlined, with just the outline pecked into the rock.

Southwestern Wyoming

Fort Bridger

Point of Rocks Station and Cemetery

The *Point of Rocks Stagecoach Station* is located right off of a busy interstate highway, but it still appears isolated, just as it must have in the late 1800s when it served travelers on the Overland Trail.

It was also an important supply point for the gold mines in South Pass City.

Next to the station there is a small cemetery containing victims who were murdered during a stagecoach robbery in the 1800s. Moulton

How to get to Point of Rocks Station and cemetery:

The Point of Rocks Stage Station and Cemetery are located off Interstate 80 at Point of Rocks, in Sweetwater County.

Kemmerer

The town of **Kemmerer** has outstanding **Fossil Butte** with unusual fossils, including entire walls of turtle and fish fossils. It also has the most extensive collection of plant fossils I have ever seen.

The fossils are arranged artistically, making them both informative and beautiful to look at. A favorite is the freshwater stingray.

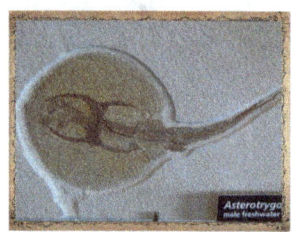

Another favorite is a wonderful bat fossil, which I've never seen anywhere else.

When you go to Kemmerer, don't miss out on the opportunity to find your own fossils at the **American Fossil Quarry**. You crack open slabs of sandstone to reveal some amazing fish fossils. I highly recommend it.

How to get to Fossil Butte and
American Fossil Quarry:

Fossil Butte is located at 864 Chicken Creek Road, in Kemmerer.

American Fossil Quarry is located at South, Farm Field Rd, in Kemmerer.

Fort Bridger

Fort Bridger was established by Jim Bridger and Louis Vasquez in 1843 to supply emigrants along the Oregon Trail. Fur traders looking for beaver pelts came in the early 1800s, but as the beaver became less plentiful, Jim Bridger left fur trading and started the trading post along the Emigrant trail to the West Coast.

Mormons began arriving in the area in 1847, resulting in conflict with the mountain men over controlling the toll ferries crossing the river.

Mormons would later own the fort in the 1850s before it became a military fort in 1858. The military abandoned the fort in 1890. Varney, Wyoming Parks

Some of the more famous visitors to Fort Bridger were James and Margaret Reed of the Donner Party, who arrived in July, 1846. They purchased two oxen before making their way west.

As you walk around the fort, look out for the *Grave of Thornburgh*, the *Pony Express barn*, *post traders store*, *mess hall*, and *warehouse*.

You will also see the two-story *Commanding officers quarters* built in 1884, and additional officer's quarters built in the 1880s.

The barracks, built in the 1880s is now a **Visitor's Center**, with a fascinating collection of artifacts. My favorites are a shirt worn by Jim Bridger and assorted surgical instruments.

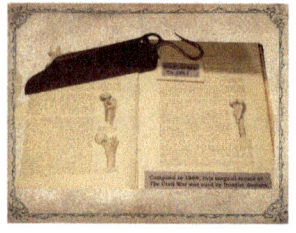

Don't miss the bone saw and anatomy book, frightening relics of Civil War medicine from 1869.

How to get to Fort Bridger:

Fort Bridger is located 3 miles south of exit 34, off of Interstate 80.

Profiles in history:

The story of ***Thornburgh*** is the story of a heroic canine. The little puppy, later named Thornburgh, was found at the scene of a massacre in 1879. Ute Indians killed the soldiers, but the puppy was spared. He got his name from Major Thornburgh, who led his troops and died in the massacre.

The little puppy grew into an adult dog, with the help of the soldiers at Fort Bridger. Thornburgh was adopted by a teamster, named Buchanan, "Buck" who befriended the dog. Thornburgh was viciously kicked by a mule, so Buck placed Thornburgh in his own bunk and nursed him. During his life, Thornburgh caught a would-be thief stealing supplies, warned of an Indian attack, broke up a knife fight, and saved a boy from drowning. You can see Thornburgh at the far right in this photograph.

Thornburgh died September 27th, 1888 and is buried in a white picket enclosure at Ft. Bridger with a headstone that reads: *"Man never had a better, truer, braver friend. Sleep on, old fellow, we'll meet again across the range."* Fort Bridger Historical Association

A word about the fossil bone wars:

The area of Fort Bridger was part of the *fossil bone wars* in the 1860s, when bones from extinct mammals from the Eocene period were discovered. The bones were nearly 50 million years old.

Some of the bones were shipped to Yale University, including an ancient horse, known as orohippus, which was discovered in 1871. Over 67 genera of mammals and turtles, lizards, crocodiles, and fish were shipped to Yale, Princeton, and the American Museum of Natural History between 1877 and 1906. Dickson, Nelson

Southern Wyoming

Fort Steele

Rawlins

R*awlins** is the city which houses the ***Wyoming Frontier Prison, a magnificent building, built in 1893. Refinements including a concrete wall at least 16 inches thick were made in 1915.

These were followed in 1916 by building more structures including a bakery, dining room, kitchen, chapel, a hospital, and a death house.

Prison reforms during the 1920s and 1930s led to more opportunities for inmates, including working outside the prison, or inside the prison at a shirt factory. Prisoners could also get an education. The prison was deemed unfit to house inmates and it was closed down in 1981.

When I visited, the prison was closed for tours, but I did get to walk around with the cutest little deer that ate right out of my hand. What a wonderful experience.

How to get to Wyoming Frontier Prison Museum:

The Frontier Prison is located at 500 W. Walnut Street in Rawlins.

Ghost story:

Ann Robbins was born in the mid 1870s and lived in the Green Mountain area of South Central Wyoming. She was a rodeo queen who went by the name of Prairie Rose. After she retired from the rodeo circuit, Prairie Rose established a homestead near the town of Rawlins with her husband Charles.

During a cold winter day in 1932, Charles left for Rawlins, leaving his wife alone. The cold day soon turned into a blizzard and Prairie Rose went outside to care for her animals. She disappeared, never to be heard from again. Then, in the summer of 1939, a sheep herder discovered a skeleton, clad in rags. It was what remained of Prairie Rose. To this day, cowboys can still hear her cries across the mountains. ^{Munn}

Fort Steele

***F**ort Fred Steele* (Fort Steele) came to life in 1868, built to protect the railroad being constructed. The fort was named for Major General Frederick Steele, a hero of the Civil War. ^{Weis}

Fort Steele was abandoned after only a few years in 1886, and some of the buildings were sold off to various residents in the community.

The atmospheric site lies mostly in ruins, but it is in a beautiful setting, right along the river.

Today, you can see brick chimneys where houses and barracks once stood. One of the few buildings standing is the stone *powder magazine*, built in 1881.

You can also visit the ***Fort Steele cemetery***, a sad, untended place with a few broken tombstones and other markers. There are approximately 80 burials, some of which have been reinterred elsewhere. 1 officer, 24 soldiers, 8 children, 2 wives, and 45 unknown people are listed on a paper register at the site.

How to get to Fort Steele:

Fort Steele is located off Interstate 80, exit 228, near Rawlins.

Southeastern Wyoming

Register Cliff

Register Cliff

R *egister Cliff* is an important landmark along the Oregon Trail. The rock contains the names of over 700 settlers and explorers, and the dates they stopped there.

Some were fur traders and trappers. Others were emigrants and settlers, and still others were soldiers from nearby Fort Laramie.

The earliest date seen was from 1797, and another from 1829. Time and the elements have made those dates no longer visible.

A young man of 19, named Alvah H. Unthank carved his name in the rocks in 1850. He was an optimistic gold seeker headed for California. Alvah never reached the gold fields. He died of cholera while still a traveler along the trail.

How to get to Register Cliff:

Register Cliff is located just outside the town of Guernsey.

Oregon Trail Ruts

The ***Oregon Trail Ruts*** can be seen in many areas of the country, but the deepest and most visible ones are near the town of Guernsey. The wheels of countless heavily-laden wagons carved the ruts up to 5 feet deep into the sandstone rock. [Finch]

Some of the people who used this trail included mountain men carrying trade items during the 1830s, settlers headed to Oregon in the 1840s, gold seekers after 1849, and military wagons during the 1860s. Explorer John C. Fremont camped in the area in July, 1842.

When I visited, it was freezing cold and snowy, which gave me some idea of how inhospitable this area must have been for the pioneers in winter.

How to get to the Oregon Trail Ruts:

The Oregon Trail Ruts are located one half mile south of the town of Guernsey.

A word about the Oregon Trail:

The Oregon Trail travels across six states beginning with Missouri, then Kansas, Nebraska, Wyoming, Idaho, and finally, Oregon. Different branches of the Oregon Trail were used by groups of emigrants and came to be known as the California Trail and the Mormon Trail. The entire route was also known as the Overland Trail. Glassman

Between the years 1840 and 1866, approximately 500,000 pioneers traveled west on the trail. People died from diseases like
scurvy, dysentery, and malaria. Many simply starved. Others suf-
fered gunshot wounds. It is believed that 34,000 to 45,000 people
died along the trail, an average of between 17 and 22 lives per mile.
Of the dead, only about 200 grave locations are known, most of
which are unmarked. Many were intentionally buried in the path
of the wagons, so any signs of a grave would not be noticed. Only
about 20% of the Oregon Trail Ruts are identifiable today. [Wagner]

Voices from the past:

"Just threw my mirror way some while back. Why I couldn't bear the sight of my face no more, all over with creases and splotches. Looking so...so common. But my feet. Well, there is no escaping the sight of my feet. I watch them step after step, mile after mile. Won't fit no proper shoes." **Unknown Oregon Trail Pioneer.**

"Honore Liberty Timfret, wife of Zabel Timfret, I am. Birthed four fine girls and a son, I did. But that's forever been taken from me. My Timothy and Elizabeth fell to cholera early on. Somehow my heart hardened to sustain me. It took me quite a spell, you can imagine, but most recently the sight of graves has gone almost

unnoticed. I begged Zabel for some kind of marker to show my child's spot. "How will Jesus find them without a marker" But no amount of cajolin' or cryin' would change that man's mind. So, we buried them back there in the great nothing with nary a thing to mark the spot but the never-ending wind." **Honore Timfret, Oregon Trail Pioneer.**

Fort Laramie

The first ***Fort Laramie*** was built in 1834, by two men interested in fur trading, Robert Campbell and William Sublette. They named it Fort William. Fur trading began to decline in 1841,

and was replaced by waves of emigrants, all needing supplies.
Varney, NPS

Then, in 1849, the fort was bought by the Army and re-named Fort Laramie. It was named for Jacques La Ramie, a French trapper who came to the area in 1815, and died in 1820, possibly killed by Indians.

It became a protected haven for weary travelers on their way to Oregon, California, and Salt Lake City. Fort Laramie also became an important stage stop, Pony Express station, and telegraph of-fice.

In 1851, Fort Laramie hosted 10,000 plains Indians from nine tribes in an effort to promote a lasting peace. Unfortunately, the peace only lasted three years.

The fort was abandoned in 1890. Today, when you walk around the extensive grounds and buildings at Fort Laramie, you can visit the **storehouse**, built in 1884, **old bakery**, built in 1876, **Captain's quarters**, built in 1870, **bachelor officer's quarters** (known as Old Bedlam) built in 1849, **old guardhouse**, built in  1866, and the **post Surgeon's quarters** built in 1875.

 My favorite building is the **Fort Laramie jail,** a beautiful stone structure, with striking light blue doors and window frames.

How to get to Fort Laramie:

Fort Laramie is located in Southeastern Wyoming, about 100 miles north of Cheyenne, off State Route 160

Voices from the past:

"Our drinking water is living—that is it is composed of one third green fine moss, one third pollywogs, and one third embryo mosquitoes...(W)e strain through our teeth..." **George W. D. Evans**

"...We reached the Platte River, (and) Cholera broke out...(H)e was the first to take down with it and lived only a short time. (and) we had to make (a) rough box from planks taken out of the wagons...(We) wrapped his body in bed clothes and buried him..." **Mary Jane Long, 1852**

A moment in time:

On December 24th and 25th, 1866, John "Portugee" Phillips rode a thoroughbred horse from Fort Kearny to Fort Laramie, a distance of 236 miles. The conditions were horrendous, a blizzard, with temperatures below zero.

His goal was to bring help for the men at Fort Kearny, because the fort was surrounded by indians. Phillips and the thoroughbred reached the fort, but the poor horse died of exhaustion. There is a plaque dedicated to the horse which reads *"The Greatest Ride in History"* on the grounds of Fort Laramie.

Ghost story:

There are a lot of ghostly happenings at Fort Laramie, from doors slamming, to ghostly kerosene lamps piercing the darkness. Workers and security guards at the fort claim to have seen ghostly apparitions of cavalry officers, some of whom even spoke to them.

My favorite ghost story from Fort Laramie concerns a young woman, "The Lady in Green" who appears once every seven years. The story tells of the daughter of one of the founding fur traders, who had a cultured upbringing and was a highly skilled horsewoman. One day she went riding out alone, dressed in a beautiful, green riding habit. She was never seen again, alive anyway.

The first documented sighting of the Lady in Green was in 1871, when she was seen by a young Lieutenant from West Point, while he was out on horseback, hunting with some friends. This same lieutenant tried to follow her but could find no trace of her or her beautiful black horse. ^{Munn}

Cheyenne

*C*heyenne is part of the old west, and as luck would have it, one of the city's attractions is the ***Old West Museum.*** The museum contains a wonderful collection of rodeo memorabilia, but the real stars for me were the old vehicles including an old popcorn wagon, an ice wagon, a water wagon, and a hearse.

One of my favorites is the ***1886 bookmobile***, which was the first county library in the United States.

Another lovely vehicle is the ***Yellowstone Stagecoach***, from the 1920s. It was a popular touring vehicle to see Yellowstone National Park.

The detail on the stagecoach door is a work of art.

Another interesting vehicle is the American Buggy *"Jenny Lind"* made popular by the Swedish opera singer, or "Swedish Nightingale" as she was called. Jenny Lind used it when she visited the United States.

How to get to the Old West Museum:

The Old West Museum is located at 4610 Carey Ave in Cheyenne.

Favorite Places to Camp

W yoming is wide open, with plenty of area for dispersed camping. I loved camping up around ***Miner's Delight.*** It's a wonderful home base for exploring the ghost town, South Pass City, and other areas in Central Wyoming.

Belle Fourche River Campground near Devil's Tower, is an excellent home base from which to explore Devil's Tower, Medicine Lodge, and other sites. There are no reservations at the campground, which has 46 sites. Drinking water is available onsite. For more information, please visit ***nps.gov***

Guernsey State Park, located near the town of Guernsey, is an excellent option to explore the Oregon Trail Ruts, Register Cliff, and surrounding areas. There are 7 campgrounds in Guernsey State Park, offering a wide variety of camping options and amenities. For more information, please visit ***https://wyoparks.wyo.gov***

Random Thoughts

What History Means to Me

First, let me start by sharing with you my opinion of what history isn't. History is not a collection of random dates, names, and places for you to memorize. History is not a dry and uninteresting class you have to pass to graduate.

I believe history is a tangible thing. You can actually *feel* history in the places you go, and the sights you see. I remember walking up to the Acropolis in Athens. I looked down at the well-worn marble steps and wondered about how many ancient philosophers had climbed these very steps, thousands of years ago.

You don't have to go far away to experience the *feeling* of history. If you are lucky enough to live in an old house, you may experience history in your own surroundings. You might say to yourself, *"If only these walls could talk."*

During my travels across the United States, I *felt* history in many, many places. If you travel across the country like I did, you will *feel* the wonderful history of our beautiful country for yourself, and you will never be the same. You will discover what it means to be an American.

Why I did it and why you can too:

I decided to travel across the country by car because I wanted to rediscover America. When I first set out to explore the history of our country, I wanted to find out why America is the greatest country on earth, and what it means to be an American.

The politics of these United States was frightening at the time. Our country was polarized, almost beyond repair. Whether it was Democrats or Republicans, Conservatives, or Liberals, everyone was fighting.

I wanted to rediscover the joy of being an American. I wanted to rediscover our rich history, our unique and wonderful people, our tapestry of multicultural heritage, and our rich natural resources. I thought a road trip by car across eleven western states was a good place to start.

I have a degree in Archaeology, and a passion for all things archaeological. I love history, with a side love of paleontology. It is these three passions that I set my trip agenda around. I set out to discover the archaeological sites, history, and paleontological world of our country.

As I travel and write my books, I get asked all the time, especially by women, "What is it like to travel by yourself? Aren't you scared?" The truth is, I believe everyone should do what I did. It's a wonderful way to discover our country, and to rediscover yourself. The truth is, I'm scared not to travel. Traveling allows you to get to know yourself, in ways not possible when sitting on the couch watching TV.

We tend to spend a lot of our lives tuning out the world and our place within it. When you travel, you are quite literally forced to deal with your own thoughts, emotions, and feelings. You can discover yourself while traveling. You can come to understand what makes you who you are, and how you can perhaps become a better person. Above all, traveling gives you mental clarity to figure out how to live with intent. It's a way to guide your life, not just wait for things to happen.

Travel Tips & Stuff

What You Need to Know

How to get started:

P lanning your trip should be one of the most exciting things about it. You want to be spontaneous, but it is also very wise to plan your route, so you can take full advantage of all the time and miles you will invest.

- First, decide your passions. If you love airplanes, trains, or old vehicles, plan your trip around that. If you love gardens or architecture, seek that out as the focus of your trip.

- Next, read and research areas of the country that will let you enjoy what you are interested in.

- Make a list by state and city or town, of what you want to see.

- Take your handy road atlas and locate the areas on the pages.

- Make a tentative route plan, so you have an idea of where you are going.

Travel tip: Avoid trying to plan your trip down to a schedule of days, hours, or minutes. On a road trip, it will be virtually impossible to know where you will be on any given day. If you adhere to a schedule, you are more likely to stress out, and less likely to actually enjoy yourself, which is the whole point.

What you need:

You need to bring along a sense of adventure and a curious mind. You need to ditch the idea of always being on a schedule, and live a little more spontaneously to thoroughly enjoy yourself. Things will happen as you travel, both good things and bad things, and you need to prepare your mind and your soul for day-to-day changes.

So much of our lives are planned out. Between growing up, going to school, finding a career, marriage, kids, or whatever, people have lost much of the ability to be spontaneous. But you must take spontaneity on the trip with you, because you may make detours along the way to see something really spectacular.

So, for the practical stuff you need:

A great vehicle-I have a Honda CRV which is fabulous. It's old, a 2004, fully paid for, and will go anywhere. I see humongous RVs on the road, towing a car behind, and all I can think of is, they can't go just anywhere. They are too big. Bad gas mileage, cumbersome to drive, slow, and not agile like my CRV. So, I encourage you, if you want to go car camping and be able to go on remote dirt roads, get an agile vehicle, and Hondas are great.

Travel tip: Don't be afraid to do some modifications to your vehicle. I took one of my back seats out. (after watching a YouTube video) I threw in a twin mattress, a bit of drapery, and some netting. I also put some of those little portable light switches on the inside. I jettisoned anything I hadn't used up to that point. Don't be afraid to get rid of unnecessary stuff.

An awesome camera that you know inside and out. I use a Nikon and it takes wonderful pictures. Don't skimp on a camera, and don't think a cellphone camera is all you need, because you want the best for your beautiful photos.

A hot plate warmer-this little item was indispensable. You need a converter for it so you can plug it in to the cigarette lighter. Place your food inside it, carton and all, and then plug it in. 30 minutes for thawed food, about an hour and a half for frozen food. Boom! You have a hot meal by the time you stop for the night!

Window shades-the best ones are magnetic so you just place them against your windows and they cling to them, obscuring the view inside your car.

Portable cooler with wheels-another indispensable item that works great and is easy to move around. I use those nifty blue frozen blocks in mine.

Portable air compressor-this little gem plugs into your cigarette lighter and will inflate your tires if you have a flat. Fortunately, I haven't had to use this yet.

Portable battery charger and power bank-mine comes with battery cables and the power bank, yet once inside the case, it is small enough to put in your glove compartment. This little item, unfortunately, I have had to use, and it saved me.

Portable generator-mine came with a small solar panel, so it can be charged with solar or electricity. It has a decent battery life and also doubles as a light for night-time.

All season clothing-you never know what different states will bring for weather, so take hot weather and cold weather clothes, and a fair amount of shoes appropriate for hiking, or walking, sandals, and slippers, which are nice at night. Also take along a pair of cheap rubber flip-flops to wear in the public showers you might go into.

Your own pillows-I like my own pillows, so I don't wake up with neck cramps, especially after sleeping in the car.

Sleeping bag and cozy blankets-you want to stay warm and layering is everything.

Warm hat, warm socks, and fuzzy jammies to keep you warm for cold nights sleeping in the car.

A great road atlas, and great guidebooks-get one that's easy to read, with great pictures. For a road atlas, just get one that is easy to read.

A word about photography:

Along with a great camera, you need to have a great eye. This is easier than it sounds once you have worked with your camera and are comfortable taking pictures with it. I am not a professional photographer, but I like my pictures and other people do too.

These are my tips for taking great pictures:

- Experiment with taking both horizontal and vertical shots.

- Don't always put the subject of the photo in the middle of the photograph.

- This one is important: pay attention to the foreground,

and if possible, have something, a plant or whatever, in the foreground to help give the photo dimension and depth.

- This one is important too: turn around often to see the view you just came from. I do this quite often and some of my best pictures have resulted from when I turned around and took the shot.

You can also take a mental photo. Place an image in your mind that you can call upon later. Use all of your senses to see, hear, smell, and maybe even to taste, what is around you. You have the means to fully experience your surroundings, and that is very important to a traveler. When you take a mental photo, be sure to jot down quick little details about what you saw, heard, smelled, or tasted, so you can jog your memory later.

And last, but not least...don't be posing in front of everything, everywhere, to show that you actually went somewhere. Most people want to see themselves in your photo and be mentally transported there, but they can't if you are there already.

To camp or not to camp:

Car camping is great. I prefer it to sleeping on the cold, hard ground in a tent. I can lock the doors, put my window shades up and be cozy for the night.

That being said, for me there were some do's and don'ts about camp sites. Some people camp in a Walmart parking lot and feel safe. I do not. I believe that if you are in a busy area, you're more likely to be confronted by a nut job who may bother you. Nothing against Walmart.

Same goes for casino parking lots. Many people believe that if they are in a public place, there is less chance of someone bothering them. I don't share this belief. I believe you are safer parked out in the middle of nowhere in the dark. That same nut job who can find you in a parking lot is not about to go driving around on dirt roads to see if anyone is parked there. At least that's my belief. You may not share it, and that's fine. Park and camp wherever you feel safe.

I don't go for rest areas either because they have a track record of incidents happening to people in rest areas, especially women travelers.

So, where do I camp? In state or national campgrounds, wildlife sanctuaries, or off on a dirt road somewhere, usually out in the middle of nowhere.

There are definitely times when I stay in a motel. I use Hotels.com because I like their stay 10 nights, get 1 night free deal. So, I book a hotel or motel if:

- The weather is too hot or too cold, or too rainy

- I am in a city and plan to stay awhile

- I'm tired of camping, need a shower, or my body hurts

- I need to do laundry

‑‑◦✦◦‑‑

A word about safety:

When you are a woman traveling alone, it's critical to keep a low profile. Don't tell people you are traveling alone, where you are staying, or any other personal information.

I don't go to bars or get drunk. I'm not preaching but you are on your own, in a city or town you've never been to, and you don't know anyone, so it's not the time to lose control of what you are doing. When you are in control, you are better able to decide which people you want to get to know better.

Travel tip: If you feel vulnerable traveling alone, that's OK. Vulnerability is part of passion, and traveling is a passionate thing to do. You can put one of those family stickers on your vehicle to indicate to others that you are not traveling alone, which can help you feel more secure.

Maintain your connections:

When you are traveling alone, there is a definite sense of disconnection. It feels almost like you are the only one in the world, traveling through space and time. That's why it's critical to keep your connections to loved ones active.

Be on Facebook while you are traveling. You may not have internet a lot of the time, or the internet will be poor. Consider paying to have your phone be a hotspot. It's a little bit of money per month, but it's worth it and has saved me from being without internet. I love the convenience of it, and you will too.

Plan your journey around visiting family members or friends you haven't seen for a long time, or people that are good friends. When you see people you know, it will ground you, so you can continue traveling.

Check in by phone with loved ones. They worry about you, and it's good for both of you to stay connected no matter where you are.

Consider traveling with a pet. I started my trip with my beloved 14-year-old sheltie named Sadie. She didn't make it to the end of the trip. I lost her to bladder cancer about four months in. My Sadie was special, and I will never forget my first traveling buddy.

It took me a solid year to decide on getting another dog. I poured over profiles of rescue dogs, looking for a little buddy I could take care of. Best Friends Animal Society in Kanab, Utah, had my perfect match. I now have Rosie, an 8 year-old sheltie that looks just like Sadie and has many of the same mannerisms. Life is good again.

I highly recommend Best Friends Animal Society if you are looking for a pet. They have 3000 acres and house up to 1600 animals at one time including dogs, cats, horses, pigs, and just about everything else. The dedicated people at Best Friends are wonderful both to you, and your potential pet.

Travel tip: One of the easiest and best ways I stay connected while traveling is to offer to take a photo for someone I don't know. Many couples, families, or singles would love to have more pictures of themselves traveling. It's an easy and quick way to have a connection with a fellow traveler, and it's good manners too.

—◈✦◈—

Practical matters:

You need to have an address to send your mail to. Keep in touch with whomever is nice enough to do this for you.

You will also need to come back occasionally to register your car, vote, go to doctor visits, and take care of any other business. You can't leave it all behind, as tempting as that may be.

Bad things that happened:

Remember when I said you need to take spontaneity with you on your trip? Well, there were many times when I used my spontaneity skillset.

The government shutdown happened smack dab in the middle of my travels. That meant that all of the National Monuments were closed. I did a lot of driving and circling around.

I also did a lot of circling around trying to avoid natural disasters. I traveled through Paradise, California shortly before a massive fire happened there. I tried to travel through the area again but was pushed out by massive flooding. My latest event was camping in Canyonville, Oregon and waking up to flames creeping down the hillside. That was day one of the Canyonville fire.

Besides being driven out by natural disasters, sometimes I was driven out by rude people. Many times it was centered around my furry traveling companion. I believe there are really only two types of people, those who love animals and those who don't.

When people see me walking my beautiful, sweet, elderly dog, they either come up and pet her, or they say something harsh.

One incident was a woman, a total stranger, who came up to me smiling down at Sadie and asked how old she was. I replied, "She is 13 and a half years old." The woman replied very curtly "She needs to be put down." Sadie was walking around, alert, and happy, and yet this woman wanted me to end her life because she was old.

Speaking of animals, several times I came very close to driving into an animal on the road. I can't stress enough how many times this will happen to you, and all I can say is, be alert at all times while you are driving. When you travel a lot of miles, you will get tired, so stop and smell the roses, and try not to drive at night.

Good things that happened:

One of the sheer joys of taking a road trip is the unpredictability of it. You never know what you will see. I am originally from Oregon, and bears are not a common sight. So, while driving high up in the Blue Mountains, I looked over and saw a bear! So exciting! He didn't stay for long, kind of shy, but so cute. I love animals, so to see the rich and wonderful amount of wildlife in our country gladdened my heart.

I met many great people on my trip, from all walks of life. They were a walking, talking advertisement for our beautiful country. I smiled at them, and they smiled back. We are all Americans, and we are all part of the human race. When you meet people across the country, you realize just how important it is to get to know your fellow citizens, and learn more about how they view the world and our country.

I have to give a special shout-out to the many dedicated people, often volunteers, who staff our state and national parks and monuments. They work tirelessly to ensure the health of our natural resources, and help travelers enjoy their visit. The same is true of the many people who staff the museums in small towns and large cities. They enjoy history, like I do, and it shows in their smiles.

Along with wonderful people, I have seen an America that is spectacularly beautiful, with open prairies, majestic mountains, and crystal clear rivers. I have seen a small fraction of the history of our country. I have seen the memorials to the brave people who shaped our country. I have fallen in love with America in a way that was not possible sitting in my living room. People ask me, "would I do it again?" The answer comes easily, "Yes, in a heartbeat."

Bibliography & Further Reading

Corbett, Christopher. Orphans Preferred: the Twisted Truth and Lasting Legend of the Pony Express. Broadway Books, 2004.

Crutchfield, James A. It Happened in Colorado: Remarkable Events That Shaped History. TwoDot, 2017.

Devils Tower Visitor Guide, National Park Service

Devils Tower, National Park Service

Dickson, Ephriam D., and Mark J. Nelson. Fort Bridger. Arcadia Publishing, 2014.

Enss, Chris. Object, Matrimony: the Risky Business of Mail-Order Matchmaking on the Western Frontier. Globe Pequot Press, 2013.

Enss, Chris. Tales behind the Tombstones. Morris Pub., 2007.

Enss, Chris. The Doctor Wore Petticoats: Women Physicians of the Old West. TwoDot, 2006.

Finch, etc. al.., Jackie. Eyewitness Travel USA. DK Publishing, 2017.

Fort Bridger Historic Site, Wyoming Parks

Fort Caspar Museum, City of Caspar

Fort Laramie, National Park Service

Glassman, Steve. It Happened on the Santa Fe Trail. Twodot, 2008.

Hill, William E. The Oregon Trail, Yesterday and Today: a Brief History and Pictorial Journey along the Wagon Tracks of Pioneers. Caxton Press, 2014.

Legend Rock State Archaeological Site, Wyoming State Parks

Legend Rock, Wyoming State Parks, 2014.

Mayo, Matthew P. Haunted Old West: Phantom Cowboys, Spirit-Filled Saloons, Mystical Mine Camps, and Spectral Indians. Globe Pequot Press, 2012.

Medicine Lodge Archaeological Site, Wyoming Parks

Mormon Ferry at the Upper Crossing of The North Platte, Fort Caspar Museum

Moulton, Candy Vyvey. Forts, Fights, and Frontier Sites: Wyoming Historic Locations. High Plains Press, 2010.

Munn, Debra D. Wyoming Ghost Stories: Eerie True Tales. Riverbend, 2008.

Old Trail Town Site, A Guide to Old Trail Town

Rutter, Michael. Bedside Book of Bad Girls: Outlaw Women of the American West. Farcountry Press, 2008.

Scott, Robert. Plain Enemies: Best True Stories of the Frontier West. Caxton Printers, 1995.

Smith, B. Ghost Stories of the Rocky Mountains. Lone Pine Pub., 1999.

South Pass City State Historic Site, Friends of South Pass City

South Pass City Walking Guide, Friends of South Pass

Thornburgh, Fort Bridger Historical Association, 0AD.

Varney, Philip. Ghost Towns of the Mountain West: Your Guide to the Hidden History and Old West Haunts of Colorado, Wyoming, Idaho, Montana, Utah, and Nevada. MBI Pub. Co. and Voyageur Press, 2010.

Wagner, Tricia Martineau. It Happened on the Oregon Trail: Re-markable Events That Shaped History. GPP, 2014.

Index

Referenced by Sections

About the Author

Julie Bettendorf is a world traveler with a degree in archaeology and a background in history. She has traveled extensively throughout Egypt, Central America, South America, Europe, and the United Kingdom, visiting archaeological and historical sites all along the way.

Currently, Julie is traveling around the US visiting ghost towns, ancient rock art sites, and archaeological wonders as part of research for her ongoing historical travel series entitled ***Wandering Woman***. Wandering Woman is a set of state-by-state guides, full of photographs, historical anecdotes, and unique tips to help other women travel and explore solo across the US by car. Julie enjoys writing freelance blogs, traveling frequently with her two adult children, and hiking outdoors with her faithful dog companion Rosie.

Also By Julie Bettendorf

Wandering Woman: Wyoming is the tenth book in the ***Wandering Woman Travel Series***. Other books in the series include ***Washington***, ***Oregon***, ***Idaho***, ***Montana***, ***Colorado***, ***Utah***, ***Nevada***, ***Arizona***, and ***New Mexico***. They are available in ebook and paperback.

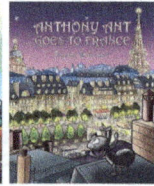

Julie has published two children's books in an ongoing, beautifully illustrated travel series entitled ***Anthony Ant Goes to France*** and ***Anthony Ant Goes to Egypt***.

She has also published a work of historical fiction entitled ***Luxor: Book of Past Lives*** which has recently been released as an audiobook, read by renowned narrator Barry Shannon.